Famous
Legends

Fairy and
Leprechaun
Legends

By
Theresa Morlock

Gareth Stevens
PUBLISHING

Please visit our website, www.garethstevens.com. For a free color catalog of all our high-quality books, call toll free 1-800-542-2595 or fax 1-877-542-2596.

Cataloging-in-Publication Data

Names: Morlock, Theresa.
Title: Fairy and leprechaun legends / Theresa Morlock.
Description: New York : Gareth Stevens Publishing, 2018. | Series: Famous legends | Includes index.
Identifiers: ISBN 9781538203538 (pbk.) | ISBN 9781538203552 (library bound) | ISBN 9781538203545 (6 pack)
Subjects: LCSH: Leprechauns–Juvenile literature. | Fairies–Ireland–Juvenile literature. | Tales–Ireland–Juvenile literature.
Classification: LCC GR153.5 M8417 2018 | DDC 398.2109417–dc23

First Edition

Published in 2018 by
Gareth Stevens Publishing
111 East 14th Street, Suite 349
New York, NY 10003

Copyright © 2018 Gareth Stevens Publishing

Designer: Laura Bowen
Editor: Therese Shea

Photo credits: Cover, p. 1 (leprechaun) Vera Petruk/Shutterstock.com; cover, p. 1 (forest) NEILRAS/Shutterstock.com; cover, p. 1 (ribbon) barbaliss/Shutterstock.com; cover, p. 1 (leather) Pink Pueblo/Shutterstock.com; cover, pp. 1–32 (sign) Sarawut Padungkwan/Shutterstock.com; cover, pp. 1–32 (vines) vitasunny/Shutterstock.com; cover, pp. 1–32 (parchment) TyBy/Shutterstock.com; cover, pp. 1–32 (background) HorenkO/Shutterstock.com; p. 5 (nymphs, pixies, and will-o-wisps) Csemerick/Wikimedia Commons; p. 5 (water sprite) Very trivial/Wikimedia Commons; p. 7 nokee/ Getty Images; pp. 9, 29 (main) Culture Club/Hulton Archive/Getty Images; p. 11 swim ink 2 llc/Corbis Historical/ Getty Images; p. 13 (main) Design Pics/The Irish Images Collection/Getty Images; p. 13 (inset) Kersti Lindstrom/ Shutterstock.com; p. 15 (leprechaun) FrancisTyers~commonswiki/Wikimedia Commons; p. 15 (Croker) Universal History Archive/Universal Images Group/Getty Images; p. 17 GraphicaArtis/Archive Photos/Getty Images; pp. 19, 21, 23, 25 (main) Bensin/Wikimedia Commons; p. 25 (inset) Searobin/Wikimedia Commons; p. 27 Buyenlarge/ArchivePhotos/Getty Images.

Printed in China

CPSIA compliance information: Batch #CS17GS: For further information contact Gareth Stevens, New York, New York at 1-800-542-2595.

Contents

Words in the glossary appear in **bold** type the first time they are used in the text.

What's a Fairy?

When you picture a fairy, you probably think of a beautiful tiny creature with graceful wings. You might be surprised to learn that this is just one of the many different forms that fairies take in people's imaginations.

Cultures around the world have created hundreds of **legends** about different kinds of fairies. Fairies may make their homes in trees, in water, or under rocks, according to **lore**. Some are wicked little goblins, and others are floating balls of light. In Ireland, leprechauns are a kind of fairy!

The Inside Story

Not every fairy tale actually has fairies in it, but something strange or magical usually happens. Most fairy tales are based on **folktales** that have been passed down for hundreds of years.

Legends tell of all sorts of different fairies. Pixies, nymphs, sprites, and will-o'-wisps are a few.

nymphs

will-o'-wisps

pixies

water sprite

5

Leprechaun Legends

Leprechauns are fairies of Irish folklore. They're usually pictured as tiny old men who like to be alone. They spend their time making shoes. They're also clever tricksters.

You might have heard that every leprechaun has a hidden pot of gold. People can make a leprechaun reveal his gold's hiding place by holding onto him. However, leprechauns are hard to find and even harder to keep hold of. And if you take your eyes off a leprechaun for even a second, he'll disappear!

The Inside Story

What we think of as leprechauns today don't appear much like they do in lore. For example, leprechauns were said to wear red, but now are only shown in green clothes.

"The Field of the Boliauns"

"The Field of the Boliauns" is an Irish legend that tells the story of what might happen if you come upon a leprechaun. Here's a retelling:

On a holiday called Lady Day, Tom Fitzpatrick went out for a walk. Tom was passing by a bush when he heard a strange sound that made him stop. Tap, tap, tap!

"Whatever could it be?" Tom asked. He looked through the branches of the bush. That's when he spied a tiny man—a leprechaun!

The Inside Story

Lady Day or Lady's Day is the day when Christians honor Mary, the mother of Jesus. In Ireland, where this legend takes place, it occurs on August 15.

All was quiet in Tom's little Irish village on Lady Day. Tom was about to stumble upon some excitement, though!

The Leprechaun's Trick

Tom had never seen a leprechaun before! He knew he must not take his eyes off him. If he did, he'd disappear, and Tom would never find his pot of gold.

"Why are you working on a holiday?" Tom asked.

"Go away and stop bothering me!" **scolded** the leprechaun. "Look, your cows got out and are making a mess!"

Tom was just about to look when he remembered—you can't take your eyes off a leprechaun! Tom grabbed the leprechaun and shouted, "Take me to your pot of gold!"

Tom knew the leprechaun would try to trick him.

11

Digging for Gold

Scared, the leprechaun showed Tom to a huge field of yellow-flowered plants called boliauns. "Under that boliaun, you'll find my pot of gold," he said. Then, Tom let him go. In his hurry, Tom had forgotten his shovel. Tom took off one red **garter** and tied it to the boliaun, so he'd remember where to dig. Then he ran home.

When Tom returned, he was shocked to see that every plant in the field had a red garter tied to it! After digging and digging, he went home empty-handed.

The Inside Story

In the days when this story was written, men used garters to keep their socks from falling down.

The leprechaun had the last laugh. He had tricked Tom in the boliaun field. "Boliaun" is another name for a kind of **ragwort**, shown here.

A Changing Story

"The Field of the Boliauns" was first recorded in a book called *Fairy Legends and Traditions of the South of Ireland*, written by Thomas Crofton Croker. Although Croker's book was published in the early 1800s, the story itself is from many years before that. Most legends in Ireland were passed down orally. That means that they were told from person to person, but not written down.

Retellings of this legend aren't much different from Croker's, but some words have changed to make the story more understandable to modern readers.

The Inside Story

Thomas Crofton Croker was born in Ireland in 1798. Although he didn't have much schooling, he read and traveled a lot. He spent his life collecting Irish songs and stories.

In some **versions** of the story, the trickster is called a clurichaune. That's another kind of Irish fairy. They're said to dress in red and have a pinkish nose!

Thomas Crofton Croker

15

All Kinds of Fairies

Myths and legends about fairies are popular in all parts of the world, though they aren't usually the main characters. Sometimes fairies are caring, but other times, they're cruel tricksters.

In folklore, fairies often appear **disguised** as poor or unwanted people. They reward those who treat them with kindness and curse those who don't. One of the main beliefs about fairies is that they have the power to give humans magical gifts. That's what happens in the story that begins on page 18.

The Inside Story

In some fairy tales, a fairy godmother is a kind, motherly figure. Fairy godmothers are interested in helping others, rather than themselves.

Fairies appear at special
times in legends, often to
test the main character
or offer them help.

17

"The Fairies"

There were two sisters named Fanny and Rose. Fanny looked just like their mother, while Rose looked like their father, who had died. Rose was sweet, but her mother and sister were cruel.

Mother and Fanny forced Rose to do all the hard work. Every day, Rose walked to the well to collect water. One day, she saw a sad old woman there. The woman begged her for a drink. Kindhearted Rose brought her water to sip. Rose didn't know it, but the woman was a fairy!

Rose carried the **pitcher** to the old woman, lifting it to her lips.

19

The fairy said, "To thank you for your kindness, I'll grant you a gift! Whenever you speak, flowers and jewels will fall from your lips."

When the girl arrived home, her mother scolded her for taking so long. "I'm sorry, Mother!" cried Rose. As she spoke, roses, pearls, and diamonds fell from her mouth.

"What is happening?" her mother asked. Rose told her about the fairy and more diamonds fell out of her mouth. The mother sent Fanny to the well, hoping her other daughter would receive the same power.

The mother was shocked to see diamonds dripping from Rose's mouth.

21

Fanny's Curse

When Fanny arrived, the fairy—now disguised as a rich woman—asked for water. Fanny was rude to her. The fairy said, "Whenever you speak, snakes and toads shall fall from your mouth!"

When Fanny returned home, she spoke to her mother. Snakes and toads leapt from her mouth. "This is Rose's fault!" the mother cried. The poor girl fled into the woods.

A prince riding by heard Rose weeping. As she told him her story, he fell in love with her. They were soon married.

The Inside Story

"The Fairies" shares some similarities with the story of Cinderella. Both were recorded by French author Charles Perrault. It's possible they're two versions of the same tale.

The prince and Rose lived happily ever after.

23

"Diamonds and Toads"

French writer Charles Perrault published his version of "The Fairies" in a collection of fairy tales in 1697. Like most fairy tales, this story existed long before it was written down.

The English version of the story came to be called "Diamonds and Toads." It was included in *The Blue Fairy Book* by Scottish writer Andrew Lang, published in 1889. *The Blue Fairy Book* was one of a series of fairy tale collections from around the world.

The Inside Story

Charles Perrault was a lawyer, but earned fame for his poetry. He rewrote fairy tales to make them easier for children to understand. Other stories in his *Tales of Mother Goose* are "Little Red Riding Hood" and "The Sleeping Beauty."

The legend of "The Fairies" is believed to have come from France.

Charles Perrault

25

In Pop Culture

Can you remember the first time you saw a picture of a fairy or leprechaun? You probably can't. From the tooth fairy to Notre Dame University's leprechaun **mascot**, images of fairies and leprechauns seem to be everywhere in popular culture.

Many of our modern ideas about fairies and leprechauns are based on how they've been shown in movies. Disney characters such as the Fairy Godmother in *Cinderella* and Tinker Bell in *Peter Pan* have shaped our ideas of how fairies look and act.

The Inside Story

The word "fairy" dates back to the Middle Ages. However, fairylike creatures appeared in legends of cultures long before that, such as those of ancient Greeks, Native Americans, and Arabs.

It's interesting to compare the fairy and leprechaun legends you know with older lore, such as the stories in this book.

What's Next?

Legends such as "The Field of the Boliauns" and "The Fairies" were created not only to entertain, but also to teach lessons. "The Field of the Boliauns" warns readers not to be greedy. In "The Fairies," readers learn that kindness is rewarded and cruelty is punished.

Myths and legends about fairies and leprechauns have changed as they're retold. How might they continue to change more over time? No matter what, these creatures will continue to make us wonder about the possibility of magic in our world.

This picture of Peter Pan and Tinker Bell is from the book *Peter and Wendy* by J. M. Barrie.

29

Glossary

culture: a people with certain beliefs and ways of life

disguised: having a changed appearance to hide who one is

folktale: a tale with an unknown author that isn't usually set in a certain time or place and that has been passed down over many years

garter: a band or strap that holds up socks

legend: a story from the past that is believed by many people, but cannot be proved to be true

lore: common knowledge or belief

mascot: a person, animal, or object adopted as the symbol of a group such as a school or sports team and believed to bring good luck

Middle Ages: the period of European history from about AD 500 to about 1500

pitcher: a large container to hold or pour liquid

ragwort: a yellow-flowered weed

scold: to speak in an angry way, telling someone what they have done wrong

version: a story that is different in some way from another telling of the story

Books

Hardyman, Robyn. *What Is a Fairy Tale?* New York, NY: Rosen Publishing, 2014.

Lynch, Karen A., and Cheyenne Booker. *Irish Holiday Fairy Tales. Volume 1.* Bloomington, IN: AuthorHouse, 2012.

Malam, John. *Fairies.* Irvine, CA: QEB Publishing, 2009.

Websites

Leprechaun Facts for Kids
www.kidsplayandcreate.com/leprechaun-facts-for-kids/
Learn more about leprechauns on this fun site.

World of Tales
www.worldoftales.com
Discover folktales from around the world on this excellent site.

Index